ECO PRINTING ON PAPER:

A Guide for beginners

By Glenna L. Combs

ISBN: 9798357461247 (hardcover)

Library of Congress Control Number: 00000000000

Any references to historical events, real people, or real places are used fictitiously. Names, characters, and places are products of the author's imagination.

Front cover image by Glenna Combs

Book design by Glenna Combs

Printed by KDP Publishing, Inc., in the United States of America.

First printing edition 2022.

Glenna Combs
105 Jerry's Rd
Manchester, Ky. 40962
606-598-7186

Grow where you are planted!

Psalm 96:11-12 ESV

Let the heavens be glad, and let the earth rejoice; let the sea
roar, and all that fills it; let the field exult, and everything in
it! Then shall all the trees of the forest sing for joy.

Index

Index (Continued)

Introduction

There is nothing as beautiful as the ability to bring nature inside and have a way to share it with others. Using flowers, leaves, and garden favorites to imprint a pattern on paper is a unique way to capture nature and share God's glorious creation with others. Beautiful greeting cards, artistic scrap-booking paper, and unique, hand crafted journals are some of the things that can be made using the techniques taught in this booklet.

I have put my techniques in a small, basics instruction book that will be inexpensive for beginners to buy and easy to understand.

I hope you will enjoy your foray into using Eco-printing to make lovely creations. If you love your garden and want a way to preserve some of the fabulous plants, this class is a fun and inexpensive way to do it. The plants are free and most everything you need is already in your home. With the step by step instructions in this book, you will be making fabulous greeting cards in no time at all.

Cards ready to mail

History

Using plant based dyes for coloring fabrics for clothing are as old as the hills. I mean that almost literally. Archaeologist found scraps of dyed fiber and sewing needles that dated back 36,000 years and at another site, a piece of woven flax was found dating back 34,000 years. From the time of the cave dwellers humans have covered their bodies for protection from the cold and heat. Nobody knows how long ago we invented woven cloth for clothing but from the earliest times, patterns and color have adorned our apparel. Those who knew how to extract colors from plants and animals were in high regard. However, until recently the dangers of exposure to toxins were poorly understood so many suffered from ailments caused by their craft. In addition, toxins were added to the environment.

Recently there has been an interest from the crafting arts community to get back to learning the old techniques for dying fibers using the gifts of nature. In the art of Eco printing, which was created by India Flint, one does not color the entire surface but makes patterns on the white or lightly tea stained background with leaves and flowers. This makes beautiful, subtle, soft colors and designs. There are several books on this subject but India flint had one of the best.

Natural Dyes

The first dyes used to color materials were taken from plants and sometimes animals. There were no "synthetic" or man made dyes before 1856. A few of the most desirable natural dyes are tyrian purple, cochineal red, madder red, and indigo blue. Tyrian purple came from a small mollusk and was worth it's weight in gold. Only the wealthy could afford it and often kings didn't allow anyone but royalty to own a garment that color. There was one problem though, it stank!

Cochineal is a red dye made from crushed cactus insects. It was introduced to Spain from Mexico. It took 17,000 dead insects to make one ounce of dye. One can see why plant based dyes are cheaper and easier to get. Madder red is from a plant found in Europe and Asia and Indigo is from a shrub that is processed by beating and boiling it's fibers to obtain the blue. Other plants produce colors as well but they are more subtle. Tea, coffee, and grass stains are just a few that we have to deal with and hardly even recognize them as natural dyes. Walnut hulls and poke berries are just a few that our pioneer ancestors used to color their cotton and flax dresses or their knit socks. The subject of dying with plants is extensive and there are many who teach the technique using plants to dye on cloth and leather.

Each bundle holds its ownd secrets, flourishing and beckoning to be opened, admired and adored.

Although we will not be dying cloth, this is an example of the beautiful colors and patterns one can get Eco-printing fabric.

How does it work?

The short answer is that you have to get a natural colored fiber to take on a hue from an outside source. Any fiber that is not synthetic, such as wool, cotton, silk, linen, leather, paper, and straw, can be changed by colors from other plants or animals and some metals. All parts of some plants can be used and may give different hues from the same plant. Leaves, bark, roots, seeds, and berries all my produce different results. There are many books written by experts that tell how to collect, process, and extract dyes and list plants that yield the best results. India Flint is a leading guru and her book "Eco colour: Botanical dyes for beautiful textiles" is extensive. If you want a detailed and comprehensive instruction manual, I recommend this book.

While some techniques taught in my little booklet can be used to imprint on fabric, you will learn a technique using watercolor paper and plants from your yard to make greeting cards that others will treasure because you have added love to the paper. If you are a scrap book maker, this makes beautiful pages on which to display your memories. Make a few pages and bind in a journal and give as a gift to a special friend who needs a hug.

Eco-printed Cards
Photo from a prior class

Why do plants make dye?

Plants have a substance in them called "Tannin". Every plant all over the world has this to one degree or another. I won't bore you with the scientific stuff but just think of a time you bite into an apple before it got ripe. That bitter taste that made you pucker was tannin. It keeps animals from eating the fruit before it gets ripe. It gives wine it's bite. They are large molecules that bind readily with proteins, cellulose, starches, and minerals. These resulting substances won't dissolve in water and resist decomposition. In other words, once they attach to another fiber, they are pretty much there to stay. The word comes from the old German word *tanna* for Oak. Oak was used to tan hides thus the name. When we use a plant to make a print or color on cloth or paper we are making the tannin bind to the fiber. There are many other uses for tannin but for our purposes we will stick to the colorful dyes. Some plants have more tannin than others. The time of year also will effect the color intensity of the dye because of the amount of tannin. Tannin is what makes flower blooms have different colors and makes leaves turn colors in the fall. Late summer is a great time to explore but any time that the plants are green and growing is good.

The mighty Oak tree from which the word "tannin" came.

Sometimes tannin seeps out of tree bark and into streams and rivers giving them a brown color.

Mordants

The kind of pot plants are prepared in can make the color different from one batch to the next because the metals can leech into the water. Sometimes a helper is needed to increase the absorption into the fibers you wish to color. This is called a mordant. These are usually some kind of metal salts. Some are toxic and some are not. Mordants help plant dyes to stick to fabric or paper. Colors vary depending on the fiber and the mordant used. Cream of Tarter is a ph buffer and softens the water for improved results. Tannic acid can be used by itself as a mordant, or to darken the colors achieved when using Alum as a mordant. Alum is the least toxic of the metallic salt Mordants. The non toxic mordants are Alum, table salt, and vinegar. Toxic ones are salts of tin, copper, chrome, and iron. We will only be using Alum and vinegar for this project. A few pieces of rusty iron or iron water can also be used for decorative effects or darkening the fibers. Adding onion peals to the boiling bath gives the paper a lovely hue. Don't be afraid to experiment with spices as well. Turmeric makes a lovely yellow. A few old rusty nails in a jar of water will give a blackish hue to outlines when the leaves are dipped in it. Copper items can also be placed in water and will give more of a greenish hue. Experiment and have fun!

Mordants help the plant dye stick to the surface you want to color

Fibers

Choosing what you want to dye or imprint is important. When using plants for dye, a natural fiber will be required. Cotton, linen, silk, and wool are all fabrics that take up the color well. Paper that is porous such as water color paper is excellent also. If you really want to get creative you can make your own paper but that is time and labor intensive so we will be using water color paper for this project. The weight of the paper should be 140 pound. This can be bought at any craft store, Walmart even carries it at the bigger stores. Cloth should be white and contain no other dyes as does paper.

Just remember if you try this on fabric that it must not have any synthetic threads because they will not take the dye.

Chose natural fibers such as wool, cotton, linen, silk, leather and paper

Choosing plants & keeping records

Part of the fun and joy of this techniques is gathering the flowers and leaves that you want to use. Your yard and a country road side is a heaven of materials to experiment with. The thing about this method and natural dyes is that you never know what you are going to end up with. The most colorful flower may not leave much of a trace and something that looks pretty bland may give an awesome print. You may benefit from keeping a notebook listing what leaf or flower you used with the type of mordant and a place to record your results for future references. I'm not that dedicated myself and prefer to take whatever I get. Some plants that I know work well are goldenrod, eucalyptus leaves, rose leaves and petals, mimosa, and maple leaves. Ajuga makes a pretty pattern. Any other flower that smells good usually had more oils and tannin but even those that don't often give unexpected results. Chose a variety of both leaves and flowers and be surprised! Don't expect your imprint to be the color of the flower or leaf you use. For example, a Black-eyed Susan, although yellow and brown, will give you a purple imprint. Grab your basket and harvest what you like. We will use fresh leaves and flowers for this project.

From my flower garden
several years ago

Water

Water is water, right? Wrong! The type of water may change the colors, either making them more or less intense or change the hue. City water has chlorine and other substances that may effect your results. Well water may have mineral salts leached from the ground. Creek water may have more of the natural tannin that has run off from tree bark. Rain water caught in a bucket under the leak of your roof may be the purest. In different parts of the country, even county to county, natural stream water content will differ in the amount of natural tannin, mineral salts, and other environmentally damaging run off and chemicals as well as it's ph. I'm not saying to go to extremes on getting the best water. I use tap water myself. However if you plan to do much Eco-printing catching some rain water might be best. I suppose one could buy distilled water but that gets too expensive. If your water is hard and needs a softener you may use a little cream of tarter to soften the water so it takes color better and keeps a truer tint.

Any water works
but the best is rain water.

Work Space

Your workspace can be your kitchen but since you may be using toxic plants I recommend you have a folding table in another area or outside. Now you wouldn't want the deadly nightshade to get mixed in with your spinach! Many, many common yard flowers are poisonous if eaten. Since it is hard to be an expert on which is which, I treat all as if they are. If you are using a wood table, cover it with a plastic cloth to protect the surface from water. Those plastic picnic ones from the Dollar Tree works just fine. You will also need a source for boiling. An outside grill or hot plate can work if you want to keep everything away from your kitchen. If you really want to go native, start a fire between two rocks. I use a burner on my stove in the kitchen once I have everything packaged and bundled for boiling. Never, never, never use a pot you have processed plants for dye as a cooking vessel. Keep them stored in an area where they cannot get accidentally used for food again such as outside in a storage building. You'll need a sink or water hose if outside, for rinsing. I do use my kitchen sink but clean it thoroughly after use. Also, a leak proof garbage can with a plastic liner for the vegetation refuse.

Just so you know, I don't have this fancy work table. I just use a cheap plastic folding table I can set up inside or out. But, this would be perfect for preparing the plants before placing them on the fibers and for rinsing of the vegetation at the end!

Processing Pot

You will need a rather large, deep pot to boil your bundles in. It has to be wide enough to lay the bundle in and deep enough to cover with water and allow room for a weight to sit on top without squishing the water over the rim. The material used in the pot is also important. Remember, the metal in the pot can leach out into the water and impact your prints. Stainless steel is the most leach free kind. You can also use an aluminum one but just remember the aluminum can add to the results but sometimes you may want that and it is safe. A porcelain clad pot will work as long as there are no chips or cracks. Cast iron could be used and is also safe to boil your bundle in but again, color will be different, maybe darker than you want. You have to have a rack in the bottom to keep the bundle off the bottom of any pot you use. If you have a pot without one, get a piece of rat wire and cut one to fit your pot. Have good pot holders handy too. If you don't have an old large pot that will do, go to Goodwill or another similar store and get a cheap castoff instead of ruining your good cookware. I use a large turkey roaster with a rack and it is stainless steel.

You may not need a pot this big for cards but if you choose to imprint whole sheets of paper for scrap books or plan to try this technique with cloth, then you may as well start with a big pot and only ruin one that you will no longer use to cook food in.

Supply List

Plastic gloves or garden gloves

Garden shears & Plastic bag or basket for gathering

Heat source & Pot holders

Large stainless steel pot with rack

Strong tongs

Table

Plastic table cover

Old terry towels

Paper towels, Parchment paper, thick cardboard box, strong twine

Iron

Heavy books

White vinegar

Alum (Aluminum sulfate)

Stamps with ink pads in multiple colors or chalk

Decorative edge scissors (Optional)

Roll of brown crafting paper

Fast drying glue stick, clean paint brush

Weights: Bricks, rocks, etc

Preparing your work stations

First thing is to set up your work stations. You'll need a good size table. The 6 foot folding tables are great. If you use a wood table, cover it with plastic. Fold an old bath towel in half and place on the table to absorb water. Keep a roll of paper towels handy.

Find a comfortable chair and set at the table. Place the items on the supply list close by, perhaps on a smaller table

Determine your cooking method and area, make sure the heat works. Select the appropriate pot and make a rack for the bottom if it does not have one. Rat wire can be cut to fit with a strong pair of old kitchen sheers. Any hardware store or farm supply store will have it.

Pick the weights you will use. Clean bricks, rocks, food cans filled with water or another cooking pot filled with water will do. Have them by the heat source.

Next is a rinsing station and way to collect the plant refuse.

Finally you will need an iron and ironing board or table. A table with a towel folded is best since an ironing board pad is to soft. You can scoot a large book under a towel and lay it on the ironing board if you need too. Have a pressing cloth ready also.

Harvesting Plants

Take a basket or bag out and start selecting leaves and flowers. Look for leaves that are not damaged or spotted with rust or holes. Flowers that are thick may not work well whole but can be dismantled for petals if needed. Keep in mind the size of paper you will be imprinting.

The card for this class is about 4 by 6 inches so surface area is small.

Chose smaller leaves and flowers. Imagine how they will lay on that size paper.

Flowers with pod shapes that are long and thin work well.

Chose from your own yard but include some from the roadsides. The less showy "weeds" often are really pretty on the card. Use your shears to cut the stalk clean.

You will be making 12 cards so it doesn't take a lot of plant material. However, it's better to have some to throw away than have to go back out.

Watch for ticks and bugs and be sure there are none on your plants you cut.

If you want to wear rubber gloves you can if you think you might have a contact allergy. Even if a plant is toxic it usually is not unless ingested. Do look out for poison ivy and poison oak. And, stinging worms and poison snakes! After you collect your plants, bring them in and spread out on a towel so you can see to make your selections

Mordant Solution

Place a large stainless steel or aluminum pot by the water source. Place the rack in the bottom, if it does not have one, make one from rat-wire by cutting a section to fit your pot.

Fill the pot with 1 gallon of water or more. The water has to cover your bundles. (a simple way to measure quickly is clean a gallon milk jug and fill it up) dump it into the pot Dip out one cup and put in a small cooker and bring to a boil. When it boils, add 1/3 cup of powdered aluminum sulfate per gallon of water. Boil and stir until all crystals are dissolved. Dump the dissolved solution back in the big pot. Alum is not toxic so the small pot can be used for cooking again. Alum is used in canning so it is harmless. This mordant is needed to help the plant tannin stick to your paper.

Have your weights ready at hand to weight down your bundles when they are ready. Sit the big pot on the burner and begin to heat the water. Remove 1 cup of the solution from the big pot and place it in any kind of container and take into the area where you will prepare the paper and plant materials.

Paper Prep

Get watercolor pad and tear out 6 pages. I use the 10 by 12 inch sheets for teaching purposes but you can choose whatever size you wish. Fold each sheet in half and crease the fold so it will tear. Gently tear along the fold line. Don't cut it, the torn edge is prettier and looks more natural. If you want to tear the outer edges in a decorative pattern you can but I wait until after the cards are ready to be enhances to do that. (You will learn a technique later in the course.) You will have two 10 by 6 pieces from 1 sheet.

Next, fold these pieces in half. You will have two 5 by 6 inch folded cards from each sheet, a total of 12 cards.

Next, use the small container of mixed mordant solution from the pot you have already prepared. Use a clean paint brush, dip it in the mordant and wet all sides of each card. If you wish to do it outside, a spray bottle may be used. Lay them out on your work table and prepare to apply plants.

Plant Preparation & Placement

Look at your plants and decide placement on your cards. Do you want both inside pages, and the front and back imprinted? Or do you want only one side of the card's interior imprinted, leaving a cleaner place to write? Placement is tricky for when you place a plant on one side and fold it shut, of course, the imprint will be on both sides because it is contacting both pieces of paper. You can remedy this by placing a piece of cut parchment paper between the plant and the paper on the side you want to stay clear. This is true of the outside as well. If you don't want an imprint on the back, protect it from the imprint with a parchment paper cover. Use a paint brush to apply mordant solution to all surfaces of the card.

Before you place the plant onto the paper, dip it in the mordant solution. Place the plant in an attractive position on the card. Be judicious and don't pile on to many, if you do you won't be able to get as clear an outline. In this case, less is more! When you fold it over, the print on the inside halves will be the same unless you use the parchment paper as described above. Place the plants you want on the outside front. Prepare the next card. Remember, the plants on the top of the first will also imprint the bottom of the next unless protected. Repeat this process until you have two stacks of 6 cards each or one stack of 12.

Bundles

Cut four (Or 8) pieces of heavy duty cardboard from a thick box an inch bigger than your cards on all sides. Avoid printing or logo marks. You will use two pieces on each side of your stack of cards.

Next cut about a six foot piece of heavy twine and place under the stack. Press down hard because you want to make sure all plants are in contact with the paper. Next, tie it around the bundle as tight as you can. The twine might cut into the cardboard edge and that's OK. Make a secure knot, then wrap the string long wise and do the same. With the remainder keep wrapping and tying until there are several strings in various locations on the stack. Repeat on the second stack. Take the bundles and the left over mordant to the cooking site.

Your water should be hot so be careful as you submerge these two bundles, one on top of the other in the cooking pot. Make sure the wire rack is in the bottom first. Place your chosen weight down on the bundles for compression and to make sure they stay under the water. Cook them at a full boil for at least two hours. Check often so you don't cook the water below the bundles. Prepare another gallon of water with the mordant and set aside for adding to the kettle as needed.

Stack, Tie, Press, Boil

Envelopes & Waiting

This is the time to break for lunch or a cup of tea. Next, clean and dry your work table and discard the left over plants. Get the roll of brown craft paper, a pair of scissors, and fast drying glue stick.

Cut out twelve 9 by 9 inch squares from the brown craft roll. Be very precise and use a square and straight edge. They will be wonky if you guess at it and they are not square! Place a card diagonally in the center of the square. Fold each corner in loosely around the card. Leave about an 8th of an inch all the way around the card so there is room to slide it in and out easily. Crease the folds with your fingers and then open up the flaps. Cut the gaps out of the corners.

Fold the edges of the bottom flap in making a hem. Now, fold the outside flaps to the middle, apply quick dry glue to the folded hem on the bottom flap and fold it up to stick to the side flaps. Hold securely until glue dries. Cut the tip off the bottom fold or fold it under the two side flaps so it is neat and even where the 3 flaps join. Fold down the top flap. You have room to fancy up the edge of the flap with decorative cuts if you like using decorative paper cutting scissors or hand torn edges, candle scorched, etc.

Envelope Pattern

41

Back to the Cooker!

After two hours of boiling the bundles, turn the heat off and add one cup of white vinegar to the bath. Vinegar is an astringent and will serve to "set" the colors in and prevent fading.

Wait at least 2 or three hours until the liquid is completely cool to remove the bundles from the pot. I let mine sit overnight. The longer it sits in the water, the better the imprint and more vivid the colors will be. When dying or imprinting cloth some artist let theirs sit in the water for a week before removing!

Once the two or three hours have past, put on rubber gloves if you want to use them and take out the bundles and put them in the sink or a pan for rinsing. You need something to catch the debris. The only reason you need the gloves is that the alum is drying to the hands. I don't use gloves myself.

Under running water, rinse away all the plant residue, collect it and discard. Pat the excess water off the cards with paper towel and lay them out on a towel to soak up the dripping water.

Remove from the pot & wash off debris
Blot excess water

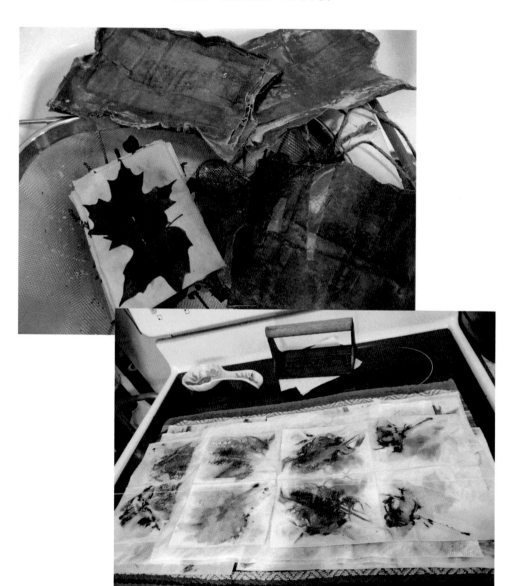

Processing the Cards

After laying the cards out on a towel to drain, pat each of them dry with a paper towel. Place pieces of paper towel between the card's pages and between each card as you stack them into a pile.

For this class, take them to your work table where we will iron them dry.

If you have time and are working on your own, you may weigh them down with as heavy book and wait a day or two to finish ironing them dry.

If you wait a couple days, replace the damp paper towel sheet with dry ones each day to help absorb the moisture.

Stacked Cards with paper towels
between layers

Ironing

Place a folded white or light towel on the end of the table and turn a iron onto high. If you use an ironing board, place a hard surface on the pad such as a large book or a board. Unfold the cards and cover with a pressing cloth and iron the card thoroughly, the longer the better to dry some of the moisture.

As the cards dry they will bend and distort unless you iron most of the water out. You can also, after the ironing, use a hand held hair dryer or lay them under a drying hood but you may periodically have to iron them again if they start to pucker. A damp pressing cloth and hot iron will straighten them back out again.

Use clean pressing cloth
to Iron cards to dry

Air Drying

Drying without an iron or other heat method can take a long time. The cards can be pressed flat with a stack of heavy books and left to dry. This may take several days or weeks, depending on the ambient temperature and humidity in your home. If they begin to pucker, a steam cloth and steam iron can straighten them back out. Replace the paper towels daily.

When they are dry enough to work with, you can start to add decorative touches such as a stamped messages, hand torn edges, and add inked or chalked colors to edges. I purchase decorative stamps from Hobby Lobby and have a whole selection of colored ink pads to embellish them with. I also have a set of paper cutting scissors with different decorative cutting blades to enhance the edges.

Stacked to air dry

Embellishments

The treatment and embellishment of your cards are as varied as your imagination. Edges can be torn by hand into rustic, ragged shapes. Another method it to char or scorch the edges with a candle flame. Decorative scissor blades can provide pretty cut edges. Stamps can be used in all color inks to inscribe with uplifting messages. The edges can be tinted with colored chalk or by raking the edge over and ink pad.

Experiment with the cards that may not look a good as you like. Use the best methods you discover on your best cards.

Embellishment (continued)
Tearing

Using your fingers, tear the edges into jagged patterns.
Use your imagination. You may want to show a peak of
what is underneath.

Embellishments (continued)
Burning

Scorch the edges using a candle. As they char, move the edge along the flame. Hold the card with a clamp so you don't get burned. Have a damp paper towel nearby to put out the flame if it produces one.

Embellishments (continued)
Cutting

Scissors with decorative cutting edges can make you
card pretty.

Embellishments (continued)
Edge Tinting

The edges can be highlighted by using chalk to tint the edges or the overall card. Also, an ink pad rubbed along the edge gives a nice finish. Ink works best in a strait edge that has not been torn or cut. Chalk worked best on torn edges.

Embellishments (continued)
Stamping

Stamps with inspiring messages are great to use. You can specialize and personalize your cards for that special event or person.

Completing the drying

After you finish embellishing your cards, you will need to do one final step. Cut pieces of paper towel and put in the middle of your folded cards and between the stacked cards to continue absorption of moisture. It will take several days for your cards to dry thoroughly even if they feel dry to the touch. The inside of the paper will still be moist.

Take this bundle home and place on a hard, flat surface and place a stack of the heaviest books you have on top and leave them for a few days to a full week. This weight will keep them pressed flat so they won't pucker as they dry. You can wait until they are completely dry to embellish if you want to.

You can enjoy your cards as they are or make a journal

The Final Step

Purchase or make a box to hold the set with their envelopes. Display on a shelf or mail to friends and family on special occasions. They will love and appreciate all the work and love you have put into each card.

Or, perhaps, you have a friend who needs more than just a card. A cute little inspirational journal would make their day. What gardener would not love to get these as Christmas gifts?

Are you decorating a room and need just the right touch on a wall. Matted and framed leaf prints in a group of four make a lovely rustic accent.

Whatever you chose to do with your cards, this is a craft you will enjoy for years to come!

Finished cards, envelopes

& journal

Making a journal

To make a rustic journal, cut the cards in half on the fold making single pages. (Should you want a larger journal, don't fold the half sheets of water color paper to start with and process them in a bigger pot if needed.)

On each page write or stamp and encouragement or bible verse if you desire. Keep the cut edges all together because this will be the spine of your journal. Keep this in mind when stamping or embellishing the pages so your message won't be up-side down!

If you have a paper cutter your edges will be more precise. If you cut by hand, use a straight edge and a sharp utility knife.

Single Pages

Cut edges lay facing each other

Make a book cover

Cut 2 pieces of hard card board ¼ inch bigger than your pages on one long and both short sides. Measure and mark using a square. Cut carefully so sides match when laid one on top of the other.

You can see that my demo is not cute very precisely but I was in a hurry so this is a do as I say, not do as I do, procedure.

Book Cover Steps (1)

Cut decorative cloth or paper 1 inch bigger than cardboard on all 4 sides. Center the cardboard in the middle of the paper or cloth with the pretty side down.

A thin brown paper bag or strong wrapping paper folds well. Brown paper can be crumpled first if you like the look. I used a thicker paper on demo and you will see that the corners don't miter well. This is also wider than an inch. Larger is OK but if smaller than an inch it won't glue down as well.

Book Cover (2)

Apply a liberal amount of roll on glue or spread liquid clue with a paint brush and paste one side of the cardboard in the center of each cover. Press down and hold until glue sets.

Book Cover (3)

After the cardboard has dried, fold the corner diagonally toward the center. then fold sides in mitering the corners. Glue in place with quick dry glue.

Book Cover (4)

Fold in all four edges, mitering the corners. Make the corner folds kiss and the corners square and neat. If they are not even toward the center, don't worry. We will cover that with another paper or cloth. Put glue on the under side of the folds and press them down. Use a heavy book to hold in place until the glue dries.

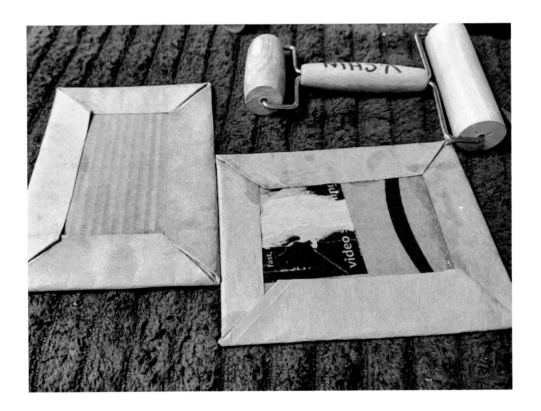

Book Cover (5)

Cut decorative paper or cloth at least a half inch smaller than the book back. Place it to cover the middle and paste it over the center. This will hide any uneven edges of the outside wrap and make it neat. Once the center paper is dry you are ready to assemble your book.

Book Assembly (1)

Using a piece of paper the length of your book, measure the length and mark a line 1 inch from each end. Fold the paper in the middle and place a mark at the mid line. Next measure ¾ inches from the spine edge and mark a line with the length of the paper. Where the horizontal and diagonal lines meet draw a circle around the spot. This is your template for punching holes.

Book Assembly (2)

Using the template for placement, punch 3 holds through both covers using a hole punch or an awl. You can do one cover at a time or both at once. Just make sure they are lined up correctly.

Book Assembly (3)

Now you are ready to punch holes in the cards.
Measure the center point of your cards on the cut or
spine side. Place the center hole from your template
over this mark. This should leave the hole on the ends
a bit closer to the edge of the cards but still far
enough away to hold. The book cover edges should
extend past the pages on the top, bottom, and front
side once assembled.

Stack the cover and cards, with the cards between the
covers. Line up the holes. Using a large eyed needle and
some heavy string, such as jute, thread the needle with
a 12 inch piece and use the needle to pull it through
the holes. Leave the tails hanging out both sides.
Repeat on the other holes.

At this stage, if you want it to really look professional you can add grommets to the book cover holes. This will also protect them and make the book last longer, look better, and open smoother.

Book Assembly (4)

Now, lay your book open to the middle page with the pages face down and the backs facing you. Have the spine pages of both sides kissing but not to tight. Laying in that position, tie the three sets of cords into double knots. Your rustic journal or inspiration book is nearly done!

Would you like a closure?

Making a closure

Make two holes about 3·4 inch apart, facing each other on both sides of the two covers.

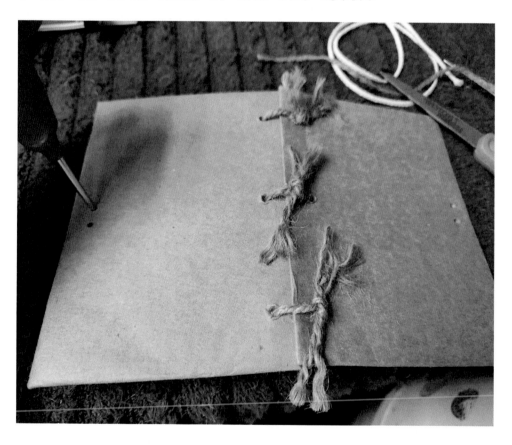

Closure (Continued)

Use stout thread to sew the button on the front cover by a needle through the two holes in the front. Tied in a double knot underneath the cover and clip the ends.

Closure (Continued)

Use the needle to thread two or three twine or jute strings from the inside to the out through both holes on the back cover. The tail of the thread need to be on the top side of the folded book. Next, tie all three strands to the other three in a double knot. If you like, beads can be tied on the ends of these strings. To close the book, simply bring the 6 strings on the back cover over, twist into one cord, and wrap around the button shank two or three times.

Glenna L· Combs

Milliner, Author, Musician, Teacher & More

About the author

I was born & raised in a large family of 10 in eastern Kentucky. My father & mother, Ott & Rachel Bowling, were craftsman by necessity. Dad was a carpenter, blacksmith, gun maker & singing teacher. Mom was a seamstress, quilter, gardener and homemaker. She excelled in needle crafts. Together, they provided a good life for their family.

In this modern age, those skills are no longer needed for survival. Appalachian living skills are slowly being lost. However, their beauty is irreplaceable. They are still taught in Folk Schools in Appalachia. Some artist have home studios where they teach. Our traditions and culture is far to precious to loose.

I started a small fiber arts home studio a few years ago and since then have had various instructors come teach their craft. I also teach a few beginning classes myself. Eco printing on paper is one. I teach other classes as well. See the list on the following page.

Classes I have hosted in the past

Felt hat shaping & finishing
Making hats with flat straw (Sinimay)
Making hats with Buckram & fabric
Carving hat block from builders foam
Hat embellishments
Felting by hand
Intuitive painting
Jewelry making
Eco printing on paper

Classes I would like to add

Basket weaving

Broom making

Corn shuck doll making

Eco printing on fabric

Paper Making

Book making

Clay pot figures

My contact information:

Glenna L. Combs
105 Jerrys Rd
Manchester, Ky. 40962
Phone: 606-598-7186
Find me on Facebook @ Glenna Combs
or at www.sycamorehollowhats.com

I teach this class as well as others.

Note

If you are interested in classes contact me.
I give private lessons as well as scheduled classes.
I have housing available for students.
Studio is small and I only take 4 at each class.
Prices vary based on the class content,
duration, supplies required, and
participation in numbers,
as well as need for housing, etc.

Blessings!